Growing up!

Trill the Fox Cub

by Jane Burton

D1341629

Purnell

A Purnell Book
First published in Great Britain in 1989 by Macdonald Children's Books
Simon & Schuster International Group, Wolsey House, Wolsey Road,
Hemel Hempstead HP2 4SS
in association with Belitha Press Limited
31 Newington Green, London N16 9PU

Conceived, designed and produced by Belitha Press Limited 1989
Art Director: Treld Bicknell
First published 1988 in the United States by Random House Inc, New York,
and simultaneously in Canada by Random House of Canada Limited, Toronto,
under the title *Fancy the Fox*.
ISBN 0-361-08170 7 (hardback)
ISBN 0-361-08171 5 (paperback)

Printed in Great Britain by Eagle Press Plc

With thanks to Hydestile Wildlife Hospital for all their help.

A vixen has had her fox cubs in an underground nest. They are three days old. Their bright pink noses are just beginning to go dark. When they are two weeks old, the cubs' eyes and ears will open, but they still sleep most of the time. The vixen stays in the nest, warming and suckling them.

At three weeks old, the cubs' woolly fur has turned brown. While the vixen is out hunting, the cubs shuffle about exploring, or they just sleep.

Four weeks old

Trill comes above ground into a bluebell wood. She should be romping around and happily exploring with her brothers and sisters. But the cubs are not happy, nor are they at all playful. Their mother has not returned with food for them for three whole days. Something terrible must have happened to keep her away. She would never desert her cubs. She must be dead.

The cubs are starving. They gnaw old feathers and twigs, because they are so hungry. Instead of playing, Trill really fights with her smaller sister. They are too young to hunt for themselves. Without food, they will die.

But the cubs are lucky. They are found and taken to an animal hospital. Trill gobbles up her first proper food for days.

Five weeks old

The cubs are in a messy, smelly state. Every time Trill fought with a brother or sister, they rolled in muck. They were so hungry, at each mealtime they got right into their bowls in their eagerness and covered themselves with food. Now that they are less hungry and feeling better, it is time for a bath. Although the water is warm, Trill is not very happy at being wet. But she is soon wrapped in a warm towel. Her woolly coat dries all clean and fluffy, and she smells quite nice again.

Six weeks old

Trill's brother Tag and sister Foxtrot get on well. They play happily together and sleep all curled up in their own hutch. But Trill still fights with them whenever she can. She is the biggest and would hurt them, so she has to be kept away from them.

When the weather is fine, Trill has fun in the garden. She is the tamest of the cubs, but is not being brought up as a pet. It is better for a wild animal like Trill to go back to the wild when she is old enough.

Seven weeks old

When Trill sees Jack the dog she is really pleased.
She runs up to him, wagging her tail and going
trill, trill, trill! Jack wags his tail too, and licks
Trill's ear.

Jack and Trill would like to be friends and play
together. But, one day, Trill will go back to the
woods and be a wild fox. She must not be allowed
to grow up thinking that all dogs are as friendly
as Jack.

Nine weeks old

At last, Trill has stopped being horrible to her brother and sister. She allows Tag to greet her in a friendly way by putting his nose inside her lip. Now all three cubs often play together with hardly any real fighting.

A favourite game is King-of-the-Castle. Anything will do as a 'castle'; today it is a rug. One cub lies on the rug being 'king', while the other two whizz around and try to push the 'king' off. Most often the bossy Trill is 'king', but now she and Tag are the 'dirty rascals' pouncing on King Foxtrot.

Trill has two toy mice, a yellow plastic one and a stuffed white furry one. She buries the plastic mouse in a corner of the litter tray, so that Foxtrot and Tag cannot get it. Then she settles down to chew the red felt ears off the white mouse.

Tag wants the white mouse, but Trill is not going
to let him have it. Suddenly she leaps up to chase
Tag away, leaving the mouse unguarded.
Foxtrot sees her chance and nips in to snatch the
mouse while the other two are bickering.

Ten weeks old

Trill is still the biggest and bossiest cub. Every mealtime she tries to grab more than her fair share. Instead of getting on with eating from her own dish, Trill rushes at Tag and drives him from his. Tag goes to feed with Foxtrot. Then he finds Trill's dish unattended.

Soon Trill sees him, hurtles over and pushes him aside. They shove and squabble, scattering mince on the floor. The noise is terrible. They shriek at each other as they gobble and snatch, until there is nothing left. They get plenty to eat, but Trill cannot forget she was starving once. Every mealtime she still gets into this feeding frenzy.

Three months old

The cubs spend most of their time out of doors, now they are big and strong and it is summer. They live in their own pen where there is plenty of room to play and they can learn to hunt mice in the long grass. Patty, an old vixen, is there too, but she has never had cubs of her own and does not approve of them. Trill runs up to her, wagging and trilling, but Patty gives an unfriendly snarl. Trill quickly understands that she must not bother Patty.

Five months old

In a corner of the foxes' pen is a large old tree stump. The cubs play on this stump for hours. They dig away at the rotten wood and tunnel under the roots. They climb on top of it and chase round and round at high speed.

The old stump makes the very best 'castle' of all. Sometimes Trill holds the fort while Tag and Foxtrot are the attackers. Other times Tag is 'king', or Foxtrot. The games are fast and furious, and often end in noisy play-fights and pretend squabbles.

Eight months old

The three fox cubs are grown up now and live out in the woods like other wild foxes. But every night food is put out for them because they still haven't learned to hunt for themselves.

The first frosts of winter turn the grass of the paddock crispy-white by morning. Trill is finishing off last night's food. Foxtrot is a brown streak heading back to the wild. It is lovely to see her running free. She was not born to be a pet or live in a cage all her life.

Ten months old

Trill always was the tamest of the cubs. She comes boldly back this morning and looks up appealingly for food. All those footprints trampled into the snow show that Tag and Foxtrot have been back during the night and gobbled up her share of the food as well as their own. Trill's winter coat is thick. She is a real little vixen now. In the early spring when she is a year old, she may well have cubs of her own underground in a bluebell wood.